ACKNOWLEDGEMENTS

Some of the information and ideas discussed in this fastback have been adapted from presentations made before the Fifth Annual Institute in Urban Education, held at Fordham University in the summer of 1973. I am, therefore, grateful to the following guest speakers for their contributions to the success of that Institute: Evelina Antonetty, Larry Cuban, Monsignor James Feeney, Edmund W. Gordon, Alan H. Levine, Isaiah E. Robinson, Jr., Harvey B. Scribner, John P. Spiegel, Charles E. Stewart, and Frank Sullivan. This author, however, assumes complete responsibility for the implications and conclusions drawn from their presentations, and for any misinterpretations.

M.L.B.

VIOLENCE IN THE SCHOOLS: CAUSES AND REMEDIES

By Michael Berger

Library of Congress Catalog Card Number: 74-19932
Copyright © 1974 by The Phi Delta Kappa Educational Foundation
Bloomington, Indiana

TABLE OF CONTENTS

Acknowledgements 5

Introduction 7

Causes 11
   Governance 11
   Interpersonal Communication 13
   Leadership 15

Immediate Remedies 19

Long-Range Solutions 21
   Governance 21
   Interpersonal Communication 24
   Leadership 26
   Conflict Management 29

Conclusion 33

INTRODUCTION

In Oakland, California, the superintendent of schools is killed and his chief aide seriously wounded in an ambush attack. The group claiming responsibility for these acts lists "offenses" of the Oakland Board of Education as justification for their actions and says that a "court of the people" convicted and executed the Oakland superintendent. The National Fire Protection Association reports that three-fourths of all fires in school buildings are now caused by arson. Twenty-five years ago, this figure was only 13 percent. In Pontiac, Michigan, five students are shot outside a high school in an incident with apparent racial overtones. The mother of a pupil enters a ghetto elementary school with three male friends and severely beats the female teacher of her son. A New York City pupil writes a letter to the editor in which he demands that "there should be a law against teachers striking students. . . . In my school one teacher bangs kids' heads against a blackboard if they don't know their math lesson."

These events point up the growing complexity of the issue of safety in urban schools. My concern in this fastback will be to assess the probable causes of such actions and to offer possible remedies for them. But before investigating probable causes, it would seem advisable to examine the true magnitude of the problem of urban school violence.

Unfortunately, the "experts" are not in agreement. One certainty is that most urban school systems are acting as if the problem were a very real one. For instance, in the proposed 1974-75 New York City school budget there is a request for $8,400,000 to be spent on security systems and personnel. That such a significant amount of money could be spent on what is basically a noneducational matter might be expected to outrage interested parents and taxpayers groups. However, there has been little protest. Apparently, the Gallup Poll of "Public Attitudes toward Education," which has found "lack of discipline" to be the major problem facing education in four of the last five years, is a reliable indicator of public sentiment. While equating lack of discipline with crime and violence may be imprecise from either the educator's or the criminologist's standpoint, there is little question that the two are inseparably intertwined in the public mind.

Nonetheless, some experts on school violence, such as Alan H. Levine, director of the New York Civil Liberties Union's Student Rights Project, claim that we really have no idea how much violence actually exists in the schools. For instance, reported figures are highly suspect. The mere fact that we have begun to systematically collect data has probably led to an increase in the number of incidents reported. On the other hand, many students probably refrain from reporting incidents out of fear of reprisals.

Furthermore, as Isaiah E. Robinson, former president of the New York City Board of Education, has observed, the definition of terms such as "assault" and "robbery" are so vague that minor incidents can be categorized as such. By the time a monthly report is compiled by the central administration, these incidents have been transformed into statistics without explanations. And the statistics, unfortunately, are then used to support or refute the allegation of widespread urban school violence.

Finally, even if the figures showing a significant increase in violence are correct, educators, in cooperation with the media, may have created a panic atmosphere in response to an unalarming situation. For instance, is an average of one act of violence per school per year so alarming? Is violence being used as a code word to improve the position of certain people and groups within the school system?

Despite this disagreement over how large a problem crime and violence actually is, there can be little question that violence affects school life. A climate of fear in urban schools affects students, teachers, administrators, and parents. This fear cannot help but produce psychological effects which adversely influence learning. If a girl is afraid to go to the girl's room because she might be robbed there, she will be uncomfortable all day long. If a teacher is afraid of being in the building during nonschool hours, he or she is going to pass up many opportunities to advise extracurricular activities or tutor students. Guards are going to be stationed at school entrances to prevent unwanted intruders from entering, but they also serve as a deterrent to many parents who might otherwise visit the school. Administrators isolate themselves from uninvited guests, but thereby create an unhealthy separation from staff, students, and parents. What factors, then, have caused this situation?

CAUSES

Washington, D.C., teacher-administrator Larry Cuban has observed that no one really knows the exact degree to which violence stems from the child, the home, the community, the school, or some combination of all these. It cannot be denied that urban society tends to be a violent one, and that aspects of it overflow into the school. Attitudes and behavior developed in the home and on the street are not left at the schoolhouse door.

On the other hand, it must be admitted that some antisocial behavior originates within the school and that some is reinforced by policies of and attitudes found in the school. Thus, while educators may be unable to cause immediate reforms in society, they can work on changing the behavior of people in their roles as students, teachers, or administrators. What is taught, how it is taught, where it is taught, who teaches it, and for how long can all be modified.

However, in the discussion that follows, it must be remembered that the school is never really a separate enclave which can remain untouched by the society it serves. Outside violence, changing power relationships in the community, and a morality in flux, for example, affect parental, student, teacher, and administrative views of the educational process. Nonetheless, it might be said that the schools contribute to their own problem of crime and violence in three areas: 1) governance, 2) interpersonal communication, and 3) leadership.

Governance

In most schools, students (and to some extent, teachers) believe there exists a system of arbitrary and inflexible rules and punishment. Donald H. Bouma asked a group of 10,000 junior high school students in Michigan whether they thought teachers treated all pupils alike. The results in his book, *Kids and Cops,* revealed that only 19 percent felt this to be a true statement, while fully 74 percent felt it to be false. The remainder were undecided. However, it appears that it was not the teachers so much as the educational system that was being blamed. Thus, when asked if they thought teachers were "pretty nice guys," 51 percent of the students said yes, 23 percent said no, and 26 percent were not sure.

One explanation for this situation is that students are not granted the civil rights ordinarily guaranteed to adults or to children their own age outside of school. Thus, pupils are almost always presumed guilty until proven innocent when their accusers are adults. Guilt or innocence and the severity of punishment are most often decided upon not by an impartial weighing of evidence, but rather by administrative or teacher fiat.

Similarly, students are beginning to question why there are so few ways to punish a disobedient teacher or administrator. They point out that disruptive pupils are temporarily removed from school with relative ease compared with disruptive teachers or administrators.

A second area where the students feel school is undemocratic is student government. Although most schools have their own student governments or organizations, few can claim more than a modicum of power. In most cases, the principal or some other school official retains the power of absolute veto. While one can argue that administrators should act as parent substitutes in such cases, it is still difficult to inculcate democratic political values when decisions can be vetoed by a "parent." The government that the students come in contact with the most is authoritarian and, in some aspects, totalitarian.

Furthermore, a recent study of high schools in the nineteen largest American cities found that only 50 percent of the schools had student representation on a dress code committee, 16 percent on a committee concerned with discipline, and 20 percent on an advisory committee that influenced school curriculum. Charles E. Stewart, an assistant superintendent in the Detroit public schools, has observed that this is obviously progress from an earlier period. But given the nature and degree of student unrest in the late sixties, it may not be enough of a gain to prevent resentment and hostility. If we accept the view of Irvin Block, author of *Violence in America*, violence most often originates among people who feel that they have little or no stake in the society in which they function. Thus, the statistics and situation described above should be some cause for concern among educators.

Related to the question of governance is teacher and/or administrative censorship of many extracurricular activities. For example, student anger has been voiced over limitations on the choice of assembly speakers, restrictions on the language and content of the student press, and the type and function of certain after school organizations. While it must be said that such regulations stem in large part from community and/or parental pressures, many students still blame the school for these limitations on their freedom and lash out against it.

Finally, while our urban schools are increasingly serving a lower-class student population composed of large numbers of minority group members, the control of the schools has substantially remained in the hands of middle-class white adults. As a result, the rules and regulations that are promulgated and the ways they are enforced have a middle-class bias. Sometimes a true class conflict develops in these schools, occasionally leading to violence when students become frustrated by pressures to conform to an alien life-style.

Interpersonal Communication

On one level, the problem of interpersonal communication is simply one of understanding a foreign language or English dialect. Large numbers of Puerto Ricans and Chicanos, and smaller numbers of other ethnic groups, do not speak English in their homes. Pupils from such backgrounds have language difficulties with which the contemporary urban school has difficulty coping. In addition, many ghetto blacks, while speaking English, have a vocabulary and sentence structure which differs in many respects from the middle-class variety expected of our school children. Finally, there are still significant numbers of immigrants who enter this country with little, if any, knowledge of English.

If the community has not introduced effective bilingual programs in the schools, these students have difficulty keeping up in a class of native-speaking pupils. More important from our perspective, such students may not fully understand school rules and procedures. They may unwittingly violate a rule and be punished without knowing why and consequently develop a hostility toward the school. Frequently, these students drop out of school and later manifest their anger in acts of crime and violence aimed at the institution and its personnel.

Even for those students who do not have a language problem, the urban school is more often than not a place of depersonalization. Edmund W. Gordon of Teachers College, Columbia University, maintains that frustration and lack of empathy are forms of psychological violence which can often lead to physical aggression. For instance, a common student complaint is that they are categorized by what they wear and/or how they talk, rather than on their ability and/or achievement. Although large segments of the adult population is similarly categorized, this superficial categorization is particularly harmful during the early school years when one's attitudes toward learning and authority are formed. To a degree, recent student unrest may have been caused by refusing to allow for diversity and individual dignity among children in their formative years.

Political and military events of recent years have tended to increase the polarization of certain students and faculty, particularly on the secondary school level. Beside making informal interaction difficult, such polarization often interferes with the educational process. Controversial issues are frequently ignored or given lip service because they might inflame passions on either side. Obviously, such practices do not help resolve differences.

Furthermore, the recent ascendancy of the youth culture has put a premium on being young. No doubt many older teachers and administrators feel somewhat estranged from their students as a result. Since the jargon and attitudes that go with this culture are radically different from what preceded them, communication problems between teachers, administrators, and pupils have increased.

Finally, the school itself seems to have become a more impersonal place in recent years, with decreasing teacher-student and administrator-student contact. This is partially a result of gains teachers have made in regard to working conditions. In an effort to concentrate more on the actual business of teaching, teachers have successfully demanded that they be relieved of such responsibilities as hall, yard, cafeteria, and study hall duty—the policing functions. In most cases, preparation periods have been substituted instead. While a valid case might be made that instruction has improved as a result, it is also true that teachers thus limit their interaction with students to one kind of activity only. This is particularly true in urban schools, where extensive extracurricular activities other than interscholastic sports are rare. Thus, teachers become strangers to all but their own classes, and their ability to serve as deterrents to crime and violence is severely limited.

Leadership

In the 1970s the administrator's authority in regard to discipline seems to be ill defined and to a great extent eroding, at least in our urban areas. Disciplinary actions against students or teachers must now be taken only after consultation with both the school's lawyer and the union representative. Otherwise, there is a real danger that legal repercussions will follow a poorly reasoned decision. Moreover, the issue of school safety has become a political one. Thus, certain people will sometimes exploit the fear of violence in their particular school or district to bring about administrative or curricular changes.

Part of the erosion of the school administrator's power has resulted from demands for student rights. More specifically, the administrator finds that respecting students' civil rights slows up his or her ability to respond effectively in certain situations. Student review and advisory committees on policy matters have made the administrative decision-making process more complex. It must be acknowledged that the demand for student rights, whether good or bad, has added a new dimension to the task of administration—a dimension which if not handled properly can lead to anger, frustration, and possibly violence on the part of all concerned.

Administrators are also feeling the effects of the school's failure to formulate meaningful goals for students or a clear educational philosophy. Administrators and teachers have never really been able to go beyond such generalities as "building good citizens." As a result, an increasingly worldly-wise student population searches with difficulty for genuine reasons to be in school. In a recent study of student activism, a Berkeley, California, high school student cited apathy as the prevailing mood among students. If pupils see little or no reason to attend school, they are more likely to cause isolated trouble or engage in power struggles for what spoils exist. Even those students who want to behave, to be part of the system, have difficulty. They need clear, sensible rules to counter peer pressure. Unfortunately, this is an age of transition, with students, teachers, administrators, and parents jockeying for educational power. Rules become increasingly unclear and/or consistently violated, and traditional students fall victim to the pressure of their more politically active and usually militant peers.

Administrative problems also stem from the fact that the schools have become increasingly the sole acculturating institution in our society. Both family and church seem to have lost much of their former influence in this area, so that teachers often need to promote positive attitudes toward society and education before any learning can take place. Many teachers find this task impossible and react negatively to it. They prefer to continue covering their subjects in an academic manner regardless of whether students learn the material or not. Consequently, pupils frequently view the curriculum as irrelevant, turn off, and sometimes attack (both verbally and physically) the people they hold responsible for this charade. Their attacks, in turn, often lead to more rigid control, to the detriment of both the cognitive and affective realms of learning. Thus, in Robert E. Weber's term, discipline becomes "a system-created problem."

Finally, part of the leadership problem is the relatively low number of minority group members found in positions of authority in urban schools. As a result, minority group students frequently lack adult models on which to pattern the type of behavior approved by schools. Just as important, the proportionally small number of minority group teachers and administrators in relation to the percentage of minority group students often creates discipline problems or tends to aggravate them. Without making a case for genetic differences and without accepting ethnic stereotypes, it can still be maintained that persons with backgrounds and experiences similar to their students' will be better able to empathize with and understand them. Empathy and understanding need not necessarily mean a more lenient attitude. In fact, many minority group parents have criticized the schools for allowing their children to get away with behavior for which whites would be punished. They worry that their children will not learn the social skills necessary to survive and prosper in a society controlled by a white, middle-class majority.

Minority group teachers and administrators are especially necessary in areas where ethnic tensions exist. In recent years, the ethnic population in urban neighborhoods has been known to change rapidly from being predominantly one group to another. During such transition periods trouble is most likely to take place, when the social roles of the various groups are in a state of flux. The presence of teachers and administrators from all ethnic backgrounds is likely to have a calming effect in such situations. Much the same effect might be achieved when tensions result from busing students to achieve racial balance.

IMMEDIATE REMEDIES

In this section, some techniques that have been employed to minimize the immediate problem of crime and violence in urban schools will be examined. For the most part, such techniques are aimed primarily at incidents caused by outside intruders. They do little to mitigate the underlying causes for such actions, but rather protect the pupils who legally belong in the school.

The most visible innovation has been security guards within the school. In many places they are professional replacements for city policemen, who had been stationed temporarily in schools where violence had occurred or was threatened. However, complaints from students, teachers, and administrators that the presence of armed, uniformed police within the school was inimical to a proper learning environment led to experimentation with security personnel hired and trained by the city board of education.

While the most obvious responsibility of such personnel is to keep order in school, educators are beginning to realize that with proper training such men and women might provide a type of informal counseling for students. If guards are recruited from the school neighborhood, they might be better able to understand pupil problems. On occasion, they could actually visit the homes of students for further information or serve as a liaison between school and home.

The major problem now regarding the employment of security guards is that of recruiting. While the advantages of using community people is readily admitted even by critics of these programs, they point out that such procedures often lead to patronage and inadequate screening. In New York City, for example, there have been instances of hiring guards with criminal records.

Accompanying the introduction of security guards has been the installation of electronic surveillance systems to supplement the man on the beat. Most guards, for example, are equipped with two-way radios connected to the central and/or principal's office. In addition, some schools have established closed circuit television systems which scan the entrances for intruders and the cafeteria and halls for potential acts of violence or vandalism. One high school has even equipped its 200 instructors with pen-sized transmitters. If the teacher is experiencing trouble or has observed some, he or she simply pushes a small button on the device and a signal is sent to the office.

A third way in which school officials have attempted to halt the increase in crime and violence is through legal means. Trespass laws, in particular, have been strenghtened. For example, the Detroit City Council, in an effort to eliminate acts of extortion, assault, and drug traffic on or near school grounds, has increased the administrator's jurisdiction to the land surrounding the school for 250 feet.

While it is relatively easy to keep unwanted individuals out of the building once classes have begun, the same cannot be said when thousands of students converge on the school to begin the day, and schools with double or overlapping sessions have an even greater problem in this regard. One remedy for this situation has been the introduction of student identification cards, often with photographs and class programs. These same cards sometimes serve as library cards and student activity tickets. Such multiple uses have minimized to a large extent student objections that these cards infringe on their right to privacy or represent a police state.

LONG-RANGE SOLUTIONS

The immediate measures described earlier are preventive. They do not provide remedies for the causes of urban school violence. Therefore, if one accepts as fact that ours is a violent society, and that schools are an integral part of it, then we must concentrate our greatest efforts on changing the values and attitudes of those who attend and manage our schools. We must develop strategies for minimizing the impulse toward violence and create an environment where students, teachers, and administrators can resolve conflicts peacefully.

Governance

One of the easiest ways to achieve wider input into the decision-making process, and thereby democratize the school, would be to broaden the role and power of student government. When students feel they have a say in the management of their school, they are less likely to attack it or its employees. Furthermore, if schools are to train students in democracy and the peaceful settlement of disputes, then the pupils must have meaningful forums through which to make their views known and their power felt.

While we tend to associate student government with secondary schools, it is imperative that some practice in decision making, particularly as it affects the day-to-day working of the school, be given as early as possible. Experts on the political socialization of children have frequently pointed out that while this process begins in the preschool years, it ends in effect at about age twelve—just when the student enters secondary school. Although students continue to accumulate knowledge during the teen-age years, their basic political values and attitudes have already been formed.

Student government, however, is meaningless if it is denied power. Most secondary school pupils, and not a few younger children, often recognize that a charade is taking place. They participate only because they realize the pragmatic value that such activities may have for college admissions. One has only to look at the total number of votes cast in any school election to see the tremendous apathy of the majority of students.

Discipline is one area in which pupils seem to have gained some power through the institution of student courts. As a model of our judicial system, where a jury of one's peers is required, it is a fine idea. Such courts are often an improvement over the somewhat arbitrary and capricious decisions handed down by administrative or teacher fiat, particularly in mixed cases (student vs. teacher or student vs. administrator).

The major drawback of student courts seems to be that students, like all people, can be corrupted by power. For instance, students have been known to take sides based on past friendships or for political advantage. Students also tend, ironically, to be harsher toward their peers than administrators and teachers previously were. To an extent, this may be due to the former's inability or unwillingness to see the complexity of the case. Finally, since convicted pupils are usually not removed from school, there may be instances when the guilty party will seek revenge against the jury. It should be noted, however, that these are also problems with which the adult judicial system must contend in one way or another.

Taking the legal training idea one step further, a group of Boston high school students, in conjunction with some law school students, recently suggested that rules regarding student conduct should be approved by a schoolwide referendum. Students, teachers, administrators, and all other employees would be allowed to vote. Such a measure, were it to become general policy, would allow students a voice in making rules as well as judging whether they have been violated.

Other decision-making areas in which student input might be solicited include curriculum and selection of school administration. To a certain extent, students have an effect on curriculum in any school that has an elective program. A course that cannot attract a minimum number of students is not offered. What is needed now is some type of student advisory body which would offer suggestions on what should be taught in required courses as well. From such a group teachers would receive direct feedback from their students. Teachers would then be able to offer material which was both pedagogically important and relevant to students' interests.

The proposal that pupils be given some voice in the selection of new administrators is more radical. However, it is doubtful that the views of student representatives on a screening panel consisting of teachers, parents, and other administrators will prevail. But adults can benefit from hearing the legitimate grievances and desires of students. In turn, students can get a better insight into the views of the community and staff. If we allow high school students to vote for President of the United States, how can we deny them the right to voice their opinion on the qualities they would like to see in the next principal?

Providing access to power is not only good educationally, it is politically expedient as well. One lesson resulting from the urban riots of the sixties, according to Irvin Block, was that the residents themselves were the most effective people in quelling disturbances. Assuming that this is generalizable to any riot situation, including school disruptions, it would follow that students who have been trained in the decision-making process might effectively diffuse a potentially explosive confrontation.

It should be noted that some teachers, too, find themselves outside the decision-making process when it is dominated by a small clique close to the administration. It would seem incumbent on modern administrators to seek actively the widest faculty participation possible in decision making and implementing. This will help end the problem of the disenchanted teacher who vents his or her anger against colleagues and administration by disparaging them in class and/or by supporting students intent on disturbing the established order.

In sum, as a CFK Foundation publication on discipline advises: "Procedures should be directed towards building, within the school, a more healthy organizational climate than towards helping disruptive pupils [and teachers] adjust to a less healthy one."

Interpersonal Communication

In the section on causes of urban school violence, it was noted that there were three attributes to the problem of interpersonal communication: language, depersonalization, and the generation gap. A first step in solving all three of these issues would be to create a more humanistic learning environment.

The sheer size of some of our urban schools (enrollments of several thousand pupils are not unusual) makes it difficult for the student to achieve a feeling of belonging. Such institutions need to be divided into smaller, more family-like clusters. One way this can be achieved is by experimenting with various school-within-a-school arrangements, such as minischools or house plans. Often these units are centered around common curricular interests of the students. Such minischools, with their full quota of administrative services, offer greater personalization by the simple expedient of reducing the effective size of the school. Students, teachers, guidance counselors, and administrators see each other more often, get to know each other better, and thereby learn to live with their differences. The inability to hide behind the shield of numbers forces people to resolve their conflicts.

In this context, it is significant that alternative schools have experienced a minimum of violence, regardless of where they are located, what type of curriculum they follow, or who constitutes the student body. In fact, Harvey B. Scribner claims that of the 10,000 students attending auxiliary high schools in New York City, there has not been a single reported act of violence. This is despite the fact that these pupils have all either dropped out of regular high school or been expelled, and some have criminal records as well.

Another possible method for making the school a more humane place would be to reintroduce the notion that teachers have duties other than instruction. While the chances of confrontation with a hostile student may be increased if the teacher has cafeteria, hall, or yard duty, the opportunities for really getting to know students are also multiplied. A student will behave in a much different manner in a structured classroom setting than in a cafeteria or outside school. The same might also be said about a teacher. Certain character traits and personal views expressed in unstructured settings might later prevent an explosive situation. As Edmund W. Gordon has observed: "To the extent to which we understand the individual and his needs, we can adjust the environmental circumstances accordingly."

Similarly, both parents and students need to put more pressure on teachers and administrators to get to know better the students with whom they regularly interact. Many teachers go through an entire semester without being able to recall the full names of their pupils unless they are in their assigned seats. Many administrators never leave their offices during the school day. As a result, students frequently lack any identity with the school or with the educational process in general.

Many teachers and administrators will object that it is difficult to learn the names of 150 or more pupils each term, let alone associate all of them with individual characteristics. Although the task is undeniably difficult, the dividends accruing from learning their names would be enormous as regards student conduct. The almost total lack of violence in alternative schools, where personalization is given the highest priority, seems to support this view.

Such efforts to create a more humanistic environment must be combined with more formal attempts (possibly courses) to sensitize students, teachers, and administrators to each others' wants and needs. Gordon has noted that students need to be trained how to express their needs in such a way that the staff will react positively to them. Similarly, teachers and administrators do not automatically adjust to the physical and mental characteristics of students who differ in those ways from pupils who preceded them. Regardless of the type of sensitivity training introduced, some guarantee must be built into such programs that the participants are actually modifying their behavior and not merely paying lip service to these ideas.

Finally, there should be an end to the repressive discipline procedures, especially corporeal punishment, found in some schools. There is little question that such punishment dehumanizes the relationships between students and teachers and between students and administrators. The result usually is not a change of behavior in the direction the school desires, but rather the development of anger and resentment on the part of the child. Frequently internalized, the anger may appear later as a seemingly irrational act of violence. Even if this does not take place, the existence of hostile feelings between specific staff members and pupils can only hinder learning.

Furthermore, leaders using physical force present a role model that we may not wish to pass on to students. They may be learning that might makes right, when we really want them to understand the value of resolving conflicts rationally. Also, by showing that discipline rests with adult authority, we lessen the chances that a pupil will accept responsibility for his or her own conduct. Why should they worry about questions of right or wrong when someone will tell them when they have violated some rule or social norm?

These views, however, do not seem to reflect either public or educational opinion at this time. A recent survey of administrators revealed that corporeal punishment was used in 74 percent of the responding districts. Equally significant was the finding that 64 percent of administrators themselves believed it to be an effective measure to guarantee proper conduct. Similar results have been obtained when both teachers and parents were polled on their attitudes toward physical punishment. There seems little question that, despite evidence to the contrary, most people believe stricter teachers and administrators will produce a generation of young people who will respect laws and rules as a result of this training.

Leadership

More effective leadership will require changes in both the structure and nature of the administrative process, from the state education department to the local department chairman. All levels of educational leaders must develop greater responsiveness to the needs of students and faculty.

For example, state officials might look into ending the present lock-step twelve-year march through school. While this program may be suitable for the majority of our children, sizeable numbers of potential dropouts might eventually graduate if allowed some flexibility in their course of study. We have long recognized the efficacy of work-study programs in this regard. Removed from the tension of the long school day, work-study students are less likely to become behavior problems than when their total program is within the school. In addition, outside work experience frequently motivates them in their school work. The next logical step would seem to be to allow students the opportunity to postpone school indefinitely if other pursuits seem more important at that point in their lives.

Scribner has suggested in this regard that we think in terms of a "bankroll" of educational years. Each child would be entitled to twelve, fourteen, or maybe sixteen years of education at birth. This education can be "spent" anytime he or she wishes. According to Scribner, this would relieve a great deal of pressure from the students and, consequently, from the schools. Compulsory education would no longer force the misbehaving pupil to remain in school. Furthermore, the stigma now associated with dropping out of school would be lessened considerably. As a result, acts of retaliation against the school from "failures" would be minimized.

Similarly, if students can choose when to get their education, they also ought to be able to choose where and from whom. Programs now exist in several states which allow students to receive "equivalency diplomas" by demonstrating on a series of tests their proficiency in subjects normally required for graduation. This program simply recognizes that people learn in different ways, not all of which involve the formal process of going to school. Why "imprison" a student in an institution with which he or she cannot cope when the same information can be obtained through life experiences, self-teaching, or community resources?

On the local level, administrators would be wise to remember the observation of Irvin Block: "The primary function of leadership . . . is not the maintenance of order but the maintenance of channels of communication and concerned responsiveness to complaint. Where there is responsiveness there is little need for 'order.' It is its own order. Disorder proceeds from those who cannot make themselves heard and whose real needs go untended."

Many urban schools exist as islands in the community, effectively separated from the very constituency they serve. Only when trouble flares up do parents try to influence decisions or administrators and do teachers seek parental advice. Parents ought to be involved in all aspects of the educational process. Far from weakening the power of the administration, parental involvement would strengthen it by assuring the support of the home for rules and regulations promulgated in schools.

One hopeful sign in this respect is the introduction, in theory at least, of community control of schools in such cities as Detroit, New York, and Washington, D.C. Ideally, such urban systems ought to be decentralized to such an extent that the principal and his or her school is practically autonomous. One result would be that the principal could no longer pass the buck to those "downtown." Community, staff, and students could hold the principal accountable for his or her actions—and inactions.

The successful administrator should always be alert for possibilities to use parents to solve some of the school's problems. For instance, lack of communication between students and staff could be mitigated to some extent by having parents interpret their children's needs to the school. There have been recent attempts to formalize this idea by establishing student "grievance tables" and student-faculty-parent councils. In both cases, parents serve as impartial mediators. Despite criticisms that parents are not qualified to provide such services, that they will be unnecessarily sympathetic to student complaints, and that the smooth functioning of the school will be impaired, these experiments seem to have the support of the local communities and central administration. To date, none of the predicted problems has materialized in any meaningful way.

Parents can also help create a more secure learning environment. Racial and ethnic antagonisms seem to disappear when parents find their children menaced by a common danger. The administrative problem of policing property beyond school grounds could be alleviated by organizing parent volunteers. For example, in Washington, D.C., parent patrol groups have been established to protect students as they walk to and from schools. In addition to this function, they have also begun a study aimed at discovering the safest route to school. Robert

Rice, a former staff member of the National Crime Commission, has observed that the general public believes or prefers that experts should handle the problem of safety. In pushing for parental involvement to counter crime and violence, the administrator is really exercising his or her leadership in the direction of having people take more responsibility for the protection of their family.

Conflict Management

In addition to the solutions presented above, which attempt to remedy specific educational causes of urban school violence, meaningful strides have also been taken to introduce the systematic study of values, attitudes, and conflict management and resolution into the schools.

For instance, during the last few years law-related education has grown enormously. There are now over 200 projects in this field. Traditionally students have studied the judicial system and the rights and responsibilities of citizenship in a very idealistic manner, and the questions of law enforcement and moral responsibility were frequently not discussed at all. The policeman was one of the "community helpers" studied in elementary school, but was rarely mentioned again. Such law-related education reflected the middle-class orientation of schools, where it was expected that most youngsters were law-abiding citizens. Unfortunately, such training was and is insufficient for inner-city children. For them, the policeman and the laws he enforces are less their friends than feared representatives of the white establishment in the ghetto.

Attempts are now underway, therefore, to present law-related material in a more realistic manner. In Philadelphia, for example, a curriculum package for grades K-12 is being created that focuses on the causes of violent behavior. One objective of this curriculum is to instill in pupils "their responsibility to overcome and prevent disruptive behavior." In Los Angeles, the county sheriff's department is sponsoring a program entitled "The Student and the Law." Deputies from that department actually teach in local schools as full-time instructors, with the emphasis on "telling it like it is." It is hoped that such regular interaction between students and police will foster a more positive attitude on both sides.

In these and similar curricular innovations, law is presented as an instrument that facilitates orderly social, economic, and political reform. It protects people rather than threatens them. Students are also taught to recognize and apply concepts associated with conflict escalation and resolution.

Paralleling the growth in law-related education is an increased interest in the process of value formation and attitude development. In fact, issues involving law are frequently used as exercises for clarifying values. Admittedly, public schools can have only a limited role in value formation; outside influences begin too early and last too long for the school to overcome them. This is probably good, since not all adults agree on which specific values are the "right" ones.

However, schools can certainly play a role in allowing each student to clarify his or her values, both personal and social. Hopefully, by encouraging students to examine their values, schools might help them develop skills which will enable them to recognize value conflicts, clarify them in terms of the parties involved, and arrive at some type of resolution of the problem. In addition, values education would stress the advantages of rational, nonviolent solutions whenever possible.

Perhaps the most revolutionary idea being suggested to reduce the level of tension and violence in urban schools is the introduction of professional conflict managers. Such people would act as a neutral party whose sole goal is conflict resolution in a manner mutually acceptable to all involved. As John P. Spiegel, former director of Brandeis University's Lemberg Center for the Study of Violence, has observed, not all conflicts are resolvable. Such situations may be made more manageable, however, by the existence of a conflict manager, a person who can play an effective mediating role.

For instance, conflict managers could help interested parties (students, teachers, administrators, and/or parents) organize and present their grievances. This function would be particularly significant in situations where the party was too young or too inarticulate to do the same for him or herself. Conflict managers could also help resolve communication problems caused by the

CONCLUSION

Some readers will object, no doubt, that this fastback does not seem to recognize the fact that there are some students who will remain troublemakers regardless of how the schools change. Advocates of this position maintain that removing this element from the school would reduce internal problems of crime and violence.

From one point of view, there is a great deal of logic to this argument. Figures compiled nationally by the Federal Bureau of Investigation and locally by city police consistently show that the majority of urban violence and property crimes are perpetrated by people under twenty-five. Just as significant, a relatively small part of this population is responsible for most juvenile delinquency. In Philadelphia, for example, a study of 10,000 boys revealed that 627 of them committed 53 percent of the crimes of homicide, rape, and assault, and 72 percent of the robberies.

Based on this information, it would seem logical to weed out these chronic delinquents from our schools. In reality, we have already done this. Such hard core criminals are not going to have any great desire to be in such institutions, at least as students. The truancy rate is so great in most major American cities that attendance officers long ago gave up trying to force such dropouts to return to school. While these youngsters pose a real problem as outside intruders, they are not directly responsible for internal security problems.

Thus, when advocates of the hard line approach suggest removing "disruptive" or "emotionally disturbed" pupils, it is not as simple as it sounds. First, definitions of such terms are open to varying interpretations. And even if this were not true, positive identification of such students in the school setting would be a difficult and risky business. Due to the sheer number of students, psychological and medical diagnoses would frequently have to be made by lay teachers and administrators. The latter might let biases from their own personal experiences with these youngsters interfere with their professional judgment.

Naturally, there are some pupils with genuine emotional disorders who need help. They should be examined by medical and psychological personnel before being removed from regular classes. But the number of disturbed students, however, is probably not as large as most teachers and administrators might imagine. Personality conflicts are not necessarily emotional disorders.

Finally, the causes and remedies for urban school violence as outlined in these pages are based on the assumption that a significant amount of the trouble is endemic to the system. Therefore, the elimination of particular individuals will probably not solve any problem in the long run. After a temporary period of calm, the system will push to the surface new faces acting in basically the same manner as their predecessors. The only permanent remedy is to begin to modify our urban schools along the lines indicated above. While no claim is made that these reforms are all inclusive, they and similar ones ought to produce the most significant results relative to the input of professional time and money.